ONE-DAY SABBATICAL

A 3-Step Retreat
for Everyone

JILL CORRAL

LIMINOCITY

Copyright © 2023 Jill Corral

All rights reserved. No part of this book may be reproduced in any form or by any electronic or mechanical means, including informations storage and retrieval systems, without permission in writing from the publisher, except by reviewers, who may quote brief passages in a review.

ISBN 979-8-218-24583-2

Publisher's Cataloging-in-Publication

Names: Corral, Jill, author.

Title: One-day sabbatical : a 3-step retreat for everyone / Jill Corral.

Description: Bainbridge Island, Washington : Liminocity, [2023]

Identifiers: ISBN: 979-8-218-24583-2 (paperback) | 979-8-9891743-0-0 (hardcover) | 979-8-9891743-1-7 (Ebook) | LCCN: 2023945577)

Subjects: LCSH: Self-actualization (Psychology)--Handbooks, manuals, etc. | Motivation (Psychology)--Handbooks, manuals, etc. | Change (Psychology)--Handbooks, manuals, etc. | Self-realization--Handbooks, manuals, etc. | Rest periods. | Happiness. | Creative ability. | Success. | LCGFT: Self-help publications. | BISAC: SELF-HELP / Personal Growth / Happiness. | SELF-HELP / Creativity. | SELF-HELP / Motivational & Inspirational.

Classification: LCC: BF637.S4 C67 2023 | DDC: 158.1--dc23

Library of Congress Control Number 2023945577

Cover design, illustrations, and layout by Jill Corral.

Published by Liminocity.
Bainbridge Island, Washington USA.

Use this book as a workbook.
(Just go ahead and crack the spine right now.)
Write in it.
Draw in it.
Rip out the pages.

Or!

Use it as a guide and
express yourself in other ways.

Answer its questions
with a pen
with your voice
with a paintbrush
with a dance.

And!

Use it
once in your life or
once a year or
once a month or
once a week.

Use it solo or
take friends with you
to share the day.

Anything you like.

CONTENTS

INTRO

Why This Is for You   7
The Approach   17
The Prep   29

YOUR DAY

1 **Free Your Mind** (1-2 hrs)   43
    Launch Your Day
    Disrupt Your Senses
    Write Freely
    Go for a Walk

2 **Play & Discover** (2-3 hrs)   55
    Warm Up: Glimmers
    Warm Up: Gratitude
    Step Outside Yourself
    Explore Your Persona
    Find the Sweet Spot
    Find Your 3 Whys

3 **Synthesize** (1-1½ hrs)   81
    Write a Letter from Future You
    How Might I... ?
    Celebrate & Emerge

Resources & Reference   107
About the Author   109

שַׁבָּת

sabbaticus

σαββατικός

WHY THIS IS FOR YOU

Why *not* you? Human cultures around the world have traditions that make time for pause, reflection, and renewal.

Gap year.

Sabbath.

Shabbat.

Sabbatical.

Sabbaticals have many names and can take many forms—whether it's a break taken by a student between secondary school and higher education, a religious observance and abstinence from work, or a leave granted to a university teacher or other worker for study or travel.

It comes from the Greek *sabbatikós*, and has been in usage since the late 16th century. It is nothing new, yet curiosity around it is rapidly on the rise in the 2020s.

The global pandemic changed a lot of people's expectations and habits around work and life. Many of us began looking for more flexible, healthier, or personally sustainable work lives — and just rethinking priorities and ways of living in general.

What's the difference between regular time off and a sabbatical? Your intention to come out the other side of it transformed.

Tomorrow is not guaranteed for anyone, and there is much to be gained from introducing moments of reflection and regeneration in our lives.

Hit refresh.

Who do you want be?

What do you want?

What do you truly need?

What do you love?

What decision do you need to make?

Where do you want be?

When do you want to do it?

How do you want to feel?

How do you want to grow?

A 2022 research report by *Harvard Business Review*[1] identified three broad types of sabbaticals from a pool of people from diverse occupational categories:

Working holidays.
Time off of paid work to pursue a specific pursuit, such as volunteer work or writing a novel or time with family, along with taking some rest.

Free dives.
Open "clean slate" exploration without specific expectations or goals, often including travel and driven by a need for discovery and adventure.

Quests.
Unexpected or unplanned pushes into time off, e.g. layoffs, burnout, illness — which launch navigating new paths through rest, recovery, or reinvention.

(Which of these most resonates with you?)

Wow, that all sounds great!

But.

What about time and money?!

This is THE question.

This is THE constraint.

In the modern world, the word "sabbatical" has traditionally been most associated with academic careers — though other institutions, like companies, are increasingly starting to formally (if hesitantly) recognize or allow them.

Those are, of course, best-case scenarios under highly privileged circumstances: time off without risk of losing one's bearings or livelihood.

A traditional format for a sabbatical is a few months or more — which requires an uncommon and magical confluence of having the time, financial resources, and optimal conditions. It is frankly a luxury that is not afforded or available to many.

And yet...

We all need space.

mental

physical

creative

space

to pause and reflect on where we are
and where we want to go.

And so...

I offer you this.

A simple **one-day sabbatical** that can be done anywhere you are, with everyday things.

The idea for this came from a longer sabbatical I took a few years ago. I'd waited decades to have some time *and* money at the same time and seized the opportunity, which was not without significant professional and financial risk.

And was one of the best things I'd ever done. I'd never, ever felt more myself than I did during that time.

I wrote a few online articles about it, presented at a professional conference about it, and over the years many people have approached me about it — people who then went on take sabbaticals of their own.

Since then, I've dreamed of recapturing that magic, and realized... it doesn't have to be a rarity. It doesn't need a perfect storm of external factors.

I can do it whenever I want.
You can do it whenever you want.

It will always look different, and it will always meet you where you are. And that's insanely empowering.

And you? You are a teacher, a post office worker, a software developer, a mom, a filmmaker, a dad, a retiree, a college student, an entrepreneur, a Swiftie.

Whoever you are, this is for you.

THE APPROACH

Where this all comes from
and why we'll do what we do.

In order to

free ourselves

to access

mental

physical

spiritual

creative

freedom and exploration...

the approach for this program,
is inspired by the practice of

human-centered design —

using this as a launching pad
to create a self-guided ritual

informed by complementary
creative, cognitive, and somatic modalities.

It integrates body and mind.

It values psychological safety and freedom.

It exalts play and joy.

It creates new pathways for self-agency
and ways to tell yourself
the story of your own life.

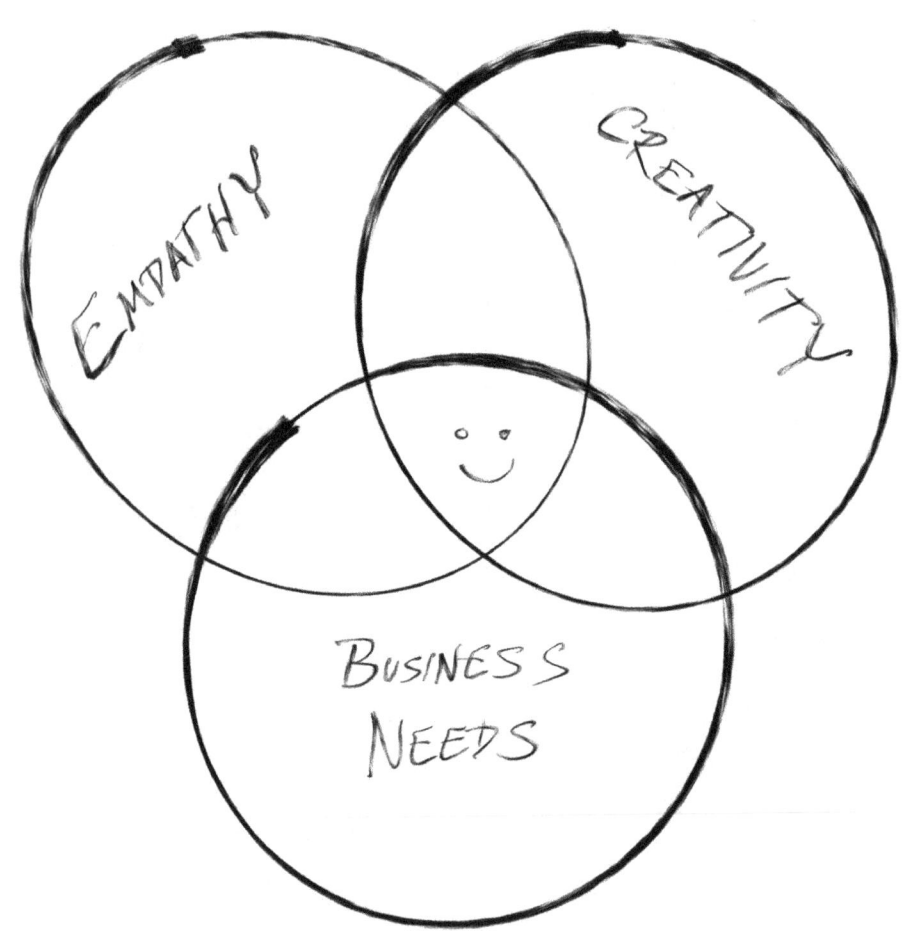

HUMAN-CENTERED *WHAT*??

I've worked in product design in the technology world for over 20 years — user experience design, interaction design, UX or UI design, and so on. (There are a million names for it and there will be a million more.) It's why the mobile phone in your hand, the checkout line at your grocery store, and the controls at your airplane seat work the way they do.

Human-centered design is the foundation for all of these, and comes with a set of approaches to observe and understand people — how they use *things* to interact with their environments and why.

What motivates them?

What are they doing? Why?

Why did they go in that direction and not the other?

What does their end-to-end experience look like?
What are the steps of that journey?

Along the way, I began to see my own life stories through this lens — and how these tools of the trade could be powerful tools for self-development and evolution.

ENGAGE YOUR SENSES

Sight.

Sound.

Smell.

Touch.

Taste.

Our senses are how we understand and experience the world — what we see, smell, hear, taste, feel. This is the information, the data that fuel our minds.

Exposing ourselves to new stimuli can powerfully impact how we feel and what we think — freeing our minds to literally feel different and to explore beyond their well-worn neural grooves of everyday life.

Think of it as sensory travel.

We will use this to...

CREATE an intentional environment where inspiration and aspiration can flourish.

DISRUPT our everyday sensory inputs with novel stimuli that enliven and ignite the mind and spirit.

PLAY with ideas, self-perception, and dreams.

CREATE

DISRUPT

PLAY

ENGAGE YOUR LEARNING STYLE

How do you best learn new things?

What type of play do you most enjoy?

Think about learning a new game or putting together a bookcase. Do you understand instructions best by reading them? Hearing them?

Do you think in pictures, words, sounds?

Do you do your best thinking while writing, drawing, walking, working with your hands?

How do you learn dance steps or how to swim? Do you like to see it step-by-step or just jump in and learn by imitating?

How do you feel most effective at getting things done?

Do you write things out?

Talk things out?

Walk things out?

There are generally thought to be three learning styles: visual, auditory, and kinesthetic.

When you are choosing how to express yourself during your day, consider your learning style as a way to make the most of it.

Here are some ideas.

Visual.

Express yourself by drawing in this book, or in a separate journal or notepad. Use different colors of pencils, markers, watercolors, or pens to express different moods or feelings.

Inspire yourself with a library book or magazine of paintings, photography, animals, or other beautiful things. Look out the window or take a walk in a new place.

Auditory.

Express yourself out loud with your voice. Record your yourself if you wish. Speak. Sing. Hum.

Inspire yourself with new music, recorded or live nature sounds. Listen calmly in a quiet room to all the sounds you don't usually notice but are always there in the background. Take a walk in a new place and take note of new sounds.

Kinesthetic.

Express yourself with movement and motion. Take a walk, dance, or stretch while thinking about the questions. Feel yourself walking in the shoes of your other selves — past or present or future.

Inspire yourself by having new objects or toys to play with during your day, or moving your body in a new way, such as with a new yoga pose or exercise or way of walking.

EXPLORE WAYS TO REST

Maybe you sleep all night and still wake up tired.

Or maybe you don't sleep well at all due to health or lifestyle reasons.

Sleep and *rest* are often used interchangeably, but it serves us well to think bigger. In her wonderful 2021 TED Talk[2], Dr. Saundra Dalton-Smith speaks of the seven types of rest, some of which we can easily bring into our day and learn to integrate into our lives mindfully beyond it. We'll be doing some deep thinking and play, which rest can profoundly support and enliven.

There are a few short and long breaks built into this one-day program. I'll offer some suggestions for them, but consider what other types of rest would be good for you, using these types as inspiration.

Physical rest.
Passive rest can be simply lying down or a taking a nap. Active rest can be gentle or restorative movement, like an easy stroll or simple stretching motion.

Sensory rest.
We live in a busy, noisy world of intrusive visuals, sounds, and constant notifications. Find peace away from the everyday chatter in quiet low-stimulation environment — or replace it with rich, soul-nourishing immersive sensory experiences like a museum or a forest.

Creative rest.
We are all creatives — creators of our own lives, homes, relationships, experiences, professions, or artistic pursuits. We can all find uplift and energy in consuming or creating music, sketches, poems – or simply by experiencing moments of awe or delight in the beauty of the natural world or human expression.

THE PREP

Plan what you need ahead of time so that you can use your best energy that day for your journey.

THE TIME

Congratulations on deciding to make space for your rest, growth, and dreams.

When will you make time for it? Will it be a weekend day? A day you already have off from work? A day you take off from work?

For those that actively provide care for others, when might you be able to reliably find another caregiver for those that depend on you?

Do you want to make time to do this once in your life, once a year, once a month?

Set a date, add it to your calendar, and let anyone you may have commitments with know that you'll be offline or unavailable that day.

Make the promise to yourself—
and then keep that promise.

I will do my sabbatical on...

THE PLACE

Everything flows from the psychological freedom and safety of your physical environment.

You should have the space to yourself. (If you are doing this sabbatical alongside others who are also doing it, you may wish to share the space.)

You should be able control the environment, i.e. access, comfort, security, ambience.

If you live alone, you can use your own space but, when possible, I recommend seeking out a new, dedicated space — a hotel, a friends' borrowed apartment, a tent in the forest, a weekend away.

Make the plan.

Make the reservation.

Make the space.

Where I will be...

THE BASICS

Give yourself the gift of few decisions and life-maintenance tasks on your day. Choose what you will wear, eat, or pack ahead of time so that you can wake up ready to go.

Wear something new or different that is comfortable and intentional. It doesn't have to be fancy, but it should be something that feels unlike your everyday self and energizes you. Consider texture, weight, how it makes you feel. It can be aspirational, elegant, wild. Borrow something from a friend or the back of your own closet, or treat yourself to something new for the special occasion.

Prepare or pack a breakfast or lunch, or plan to order in. Or take a nice assortment of favorite snacks to graze on all day. Just make it easy.

And what else do you need? Prepare those medications, pet supplies, or any other essential items ahead of time.

I will wear...

I will eat...

I will have these other essential things...

THE CREATIVE MATERIALS

All you really need is this book and a pen.

But what else could enhance your inspiration or experience of the day?

Think about your learning style or what else might spark ideas, or delight your mind and hands as you think and play.

Happy music?

Paint?

Building blocks or toys?

Nature sounds?

Crayons?

Colored markers?

A new journal?

Sticky notes?

A camera?

Clay?

I will bring...

THE SENSORY MATERIALS

We likely see the same things day to day, hear familiar music or voices, smell the same air, eat the same foods, and feel the textures and weight of the same clothing on our bodies.

Gather some materials for your day that you've had little to no exposure to before. Feel free to ask a friend or loved one for ideas, such as...

A new town or natural environment you've never been to before that has new sights, smells, and sounds.

New music you've never heard.

A fruit, vegetable, or spice you've never smelled or tasted.

A sample of perfume.

An art book.

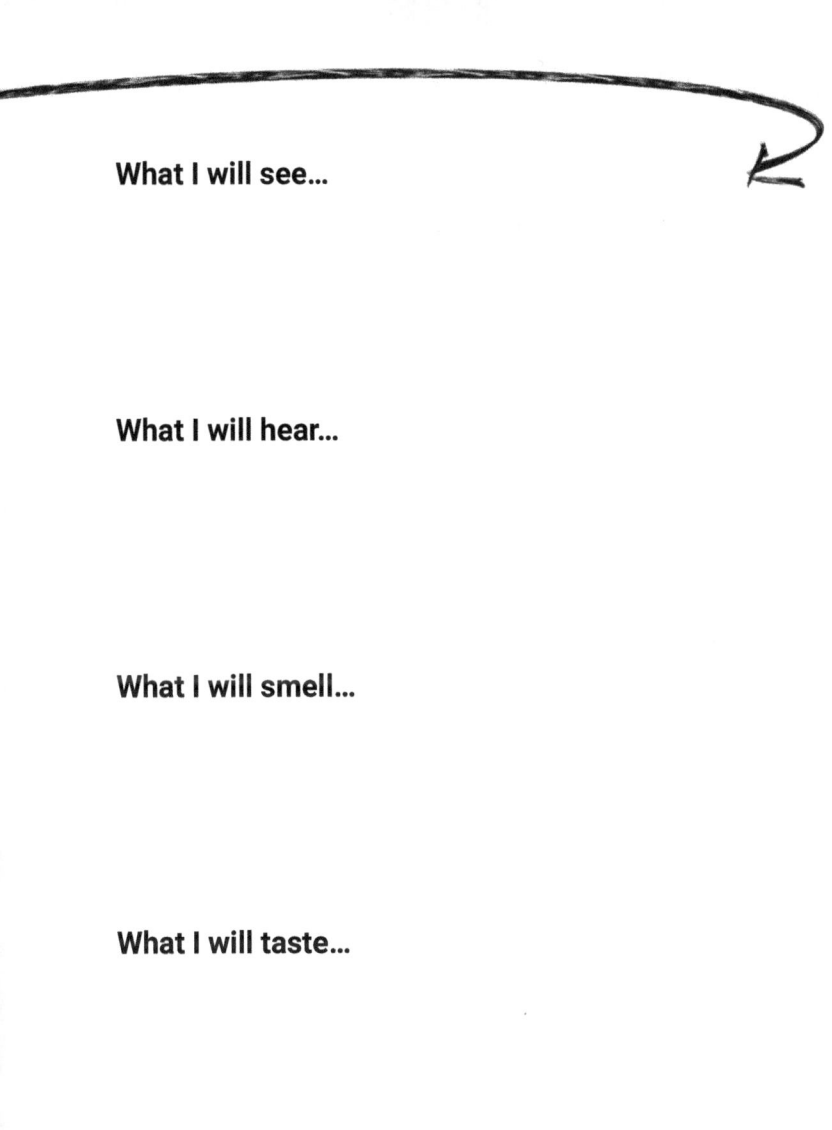

What I will see...

What I will hear...

What I will smell...

What I will taste...

What I will touch...

THE INTENTION

You may have an intention or focus in mind ahead of your sabbatical, or you may be coming in with an intention to see what direction it may take you.

Are you simply looking to relax and explore or is there something in particular you want to...

Dream about?

Plan for?

Recover from?

Meditate on?

My intention for this sabbatical is....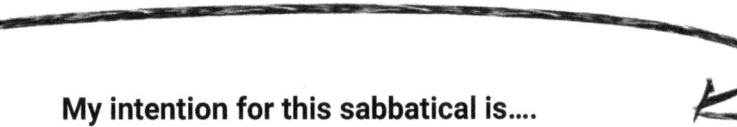

...and I intend to be completely open to what the day brings to me.

1
**YOUR DAY:
FREE YOUR MIND**
1-2 HOURS

Welcome to your day. In the immortal words of the R&B pop divas En Vogue: *Free your mind, and the rest will follow.*

LAUNCH YOUR DAY
30 MINUTES

Let's kickstart the day with a bright dynamic energy to activate our bodies and minds.

(By the way... take all the time you need or want for any activity in this book — for example, the 30 minutes given above for this one is just a suggestion. Do what feels right to you.)

Let's gooooooo!

Circle these as you complete them:

Wake up.
Good morning!

Shake it off.
Shake off the sleep like a dog or cat. Shake like you're shaking the dust off of a rug.

Dress for success.
Put on that clothing that feels new or different and like your best self.

Smile and breathe outside.
Open a window or step outside.
Smile and take a deep breath.

DISRUPT YOUR SENSES
15 MINUTES

Let's awaken our senses.

Go grab the sensory materials you prepared if you've brought them, or immerse yourself in your new sensory environment if you're in a new place.

Be curious about experiencing things in an unexpected way. Taste a tree leaf. Sniff a seashell.

Combine new sensations — like immersing yourself in new music over headphones while looking out over a new landscape or picture book.

Take a moment to focus on each of the senses as you experience the new sensation.

Look at something new.
What do you notice?

Smell something new.
What emotions do you feel?

Listen to something new.
Does it remind you of anything?

Touch something new.
Is it what you expected?

Taste something new.
Do you like it?

WRITE FREELY
15 MINUTES

Let's get the energy going!

Write whatever comes to mind in these next few blank pages. Don't edit yourself or think about it.

Just flow with your stream of consciousness to loosen up your mind, your fingers, and your inner voice.

GO FOR A WALK
15 MINUTES

Keep the energy flowing and increase your vibration with an easy 15-minute walk.

Walking awakens our bodies and minds, calms our nerves, and enhances creativity. Feel your blood flowing and enjoy the feeling of breathing and moving.

Walking stimulates both sides of the lateral body — arms and legs and eyes and brain hemispheres — left and right, right and left.

Walk outside if possible, in a green or blue natural environment. Walk past a city tree or look up at the sky.

Walk at varying speeds or paces. Try walking faster or more slowly than you usually do. Jump over rocks on the ground or cracks in the sidewalk.

Another way to effectively energize your body and mind in addition to walking (or if it's not safe or possible for you to walk), is rhythmic movement or other somatic exercise. Sit or stand in place and swing your arms or legs back and forth. Stretch your arms or torso from side to side. Move your head to look left and then right. Move your eyes or tongue side to side. Tap your arms or legs, left and right and up and down, with your hands or fingers.

Where does your body feel tight, loose, painful, good, strong?

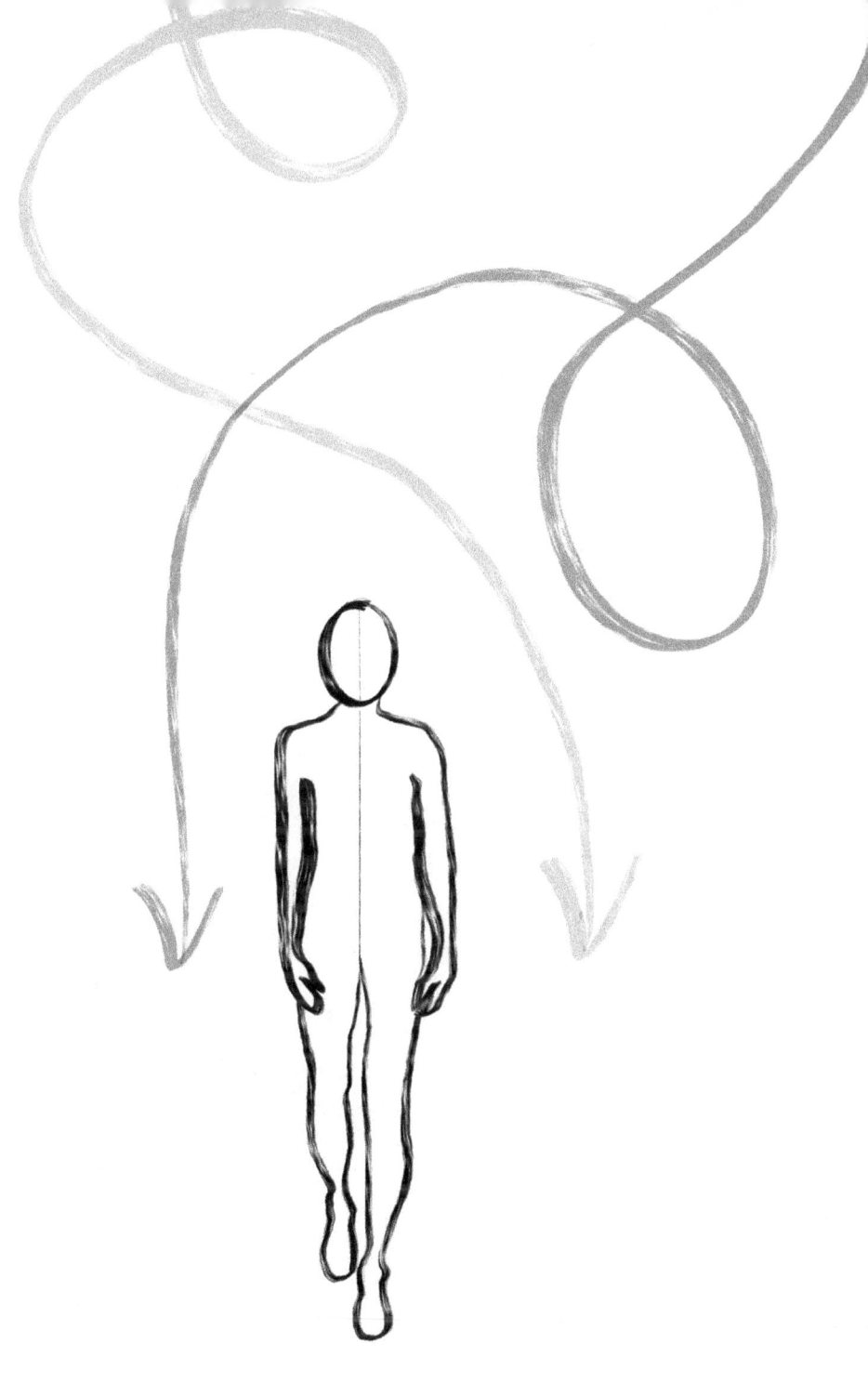

2

**YOUR DAY:
PLAY & DISCOVER**
2-3 HOURS

Go on a journey of self-discovery and dare to dream.

WARM UP: GLIMMERS
5 MINUTES

Awe.

Delight.

Sudden moments of joy and lightness that take you by surprise.

You smile.

Your eyes light up.

You feel a tingle.

Your heart skips a beat.

You laugh.

It could be your favorite song unexpectedly coming on the radio, a friendly "hello" on the street, or a rainbow.

Coined by psychotherapist Deb Dana[3], glimmers are "micro moments" in your day that spark a sense of joy and well-being. You may be familiar with the term *trigger* for something negative that takes you out of a sense of peace or safety. A glimmer is its radiant opposite.

Think of three moments of awe, or glimmers, that you've experienced in the past 24 hours — those sudden, tiny, magical moments that took you somewhere lighter and brighter.

3 glimmers I've experienced in the past 24 hours are ...

WARM UP: GRATITUDE
5 MINUTES

Our minds and bodies are by default wired to scan our environments for potential threats to our safety, usually blissfully ignoring everything that indicates or supports their well-being.

It's why we notice a headache, but not the lack of one.

It's why most news headlines are bad news and not good news.

It's why it's easier to focus on, say, the 5% of our lives that is going wrong versus the 95% that is going right.

We do, however, have considerable agency over our default wiring. We can train ourselves to seek evidence of safety and happiness, paying attention to and calling out all of our good fortune.

It takes practice — practice which richly pays off in a more positive outlook, less anxiety, and more ease in and appreciation for our lives. It's a muscle anyone can build. The more one does this intentionally, the more automatic it becomes — effectively rewiring us for the better.

What are three moments or qualities about your life that you are grateful for in the past 24 hours?

3 things I'm grateful for in the past 24 hours are...

STEP OUTSIDE YOURSELF
15 MINUTES

I am large, I contain multitudes.
— Walt Whitman, *Song of Myself, 51*

Now that we've gotten into our bodies and a positive mindset… let's take a friendly leap outside of ourselves.

We're often great at giving advice to others while being lost when it comes to solving our own problems. Or we're easily supportive and patient and kind to our imperfect friends and loved ones, while being our own worst critics.

When you see your face in the mirror, do you look upon her/him/them with kindness and love — or do your thoughts immediately turn to your perceived flaws or stresses?

What roles, identities, or personas do you contain or live as? They can be functional roles or ways that you identify or behave.

Don't overthink — just use the ones that most quickly come to mind.

On the next two pages, come up with a few personas and give each one:

Name of persona, e.g. "mom" "runner" "artist" "caregiver" "partner" "worker" "introvert" "gardener" "teacher" "people connector" "public speaker"

Quick sketch or drawing of their face, including facial expression or mood.

Main motivation, e.g. "be healthier," "advance career," "learn to dance" "improve relationship" "be happier"

Here's an example:

Athlete

Take better care of my body so I can perform better and be healthier

Who are your main personas? Try for at least 3.

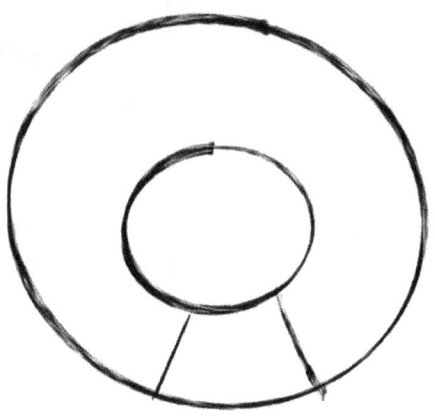

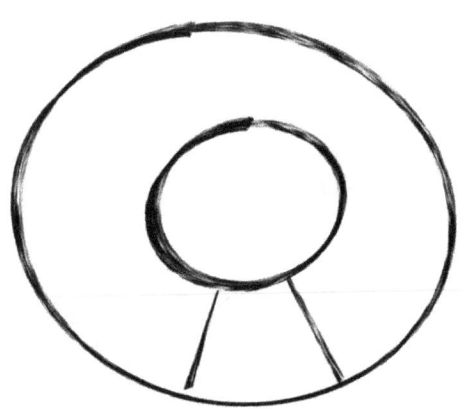

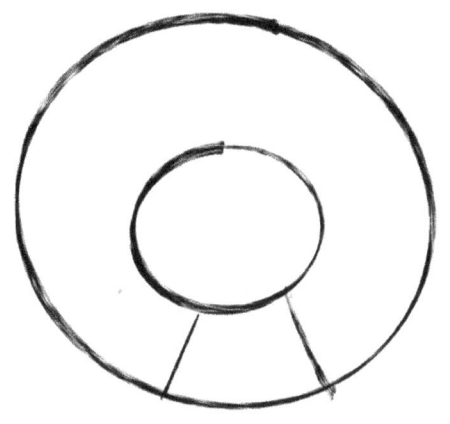

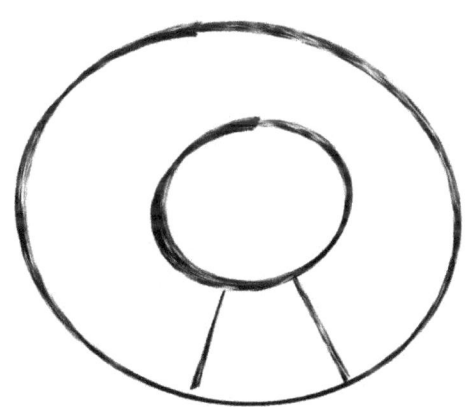

EXPLORE YOUR PERSONA
30-45 MINUTES

Which one of your personas are you most interested in thinking about and exploring today?

Choose one of them for this activity.

Imagine that you are the casting director for a TV show or movie about your life. What personal qualities would this character have?

On the next few pages, we're going to look closely at this persona and what makes them tick.

Who did you choose?

Why did you choose them?

What's the main thing that drives or motivates them?

**When are they at their best?
What situations bring this out in them?**

**When are they at their worst?
What situations bring this out in them?**

How do they feel today? Why?

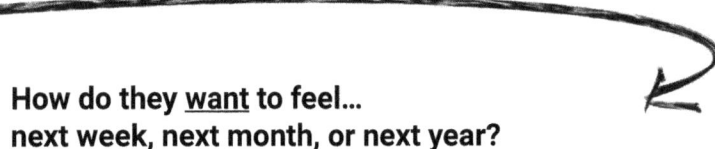

**How do they <u>want</u> to feel...
next week, next month, or next year?**

TAKE A SHORT BREAK HERE.

YOU CAN

JUMP AROUND.

CLOSE YOUR EYES.

REFILL YOUR COFFEE.

DOODLE A CARTOON.

LISTEN TO YOUR CURRENT

FAVORITE SONG

AND DO A

LITTLE DANCE.

FIND THE SWEET SPOT
5-10 MINUTES

Go back and reread your responses to those last two questions about how you feel vs. how you *want* to feel.

Think about the difference between the two feelings.

What is it?

Life circumstances?

Opinions?

Beliefs?

Emotions?

Mental?

Physical?

Spiritual?

The difference between how I feel now and how I want to feel in the future is:

FIND YOUR 3 WHYS
15 MINUTES

Now, let's do a deep dive on this.

The 5 *Whys* is an iterative interrogation method used in design thinking to find the root cause of a problem — and it inspires an interesting way to think more deeply and specifically about why we want or are motivated to do something.

It can help us to refine our vision and possibly discover a core desire that may be different from the automatic "solution" we may have previously assumed.

Go back a page and read your response to **Find the Sweet Spot**.

With that in mind, start thinking of an exploration you'd like to do or a transformation that you'd like to make in your life.

I want to explore / change / transform...

Great! Now let's go deeper.

Using what you just wrote, now progressively ask yourself *why?* Peel away the layers as you go to get to the root of your thinking.

Here's a simple example:

Thinking about what you want to change or transform...

> *I want to eat better.*

Why?

> *So that I can lose weight.*

Why?

> *So that I can fit back into my pre-pandemic clothes.*

Why?

> *So I can feel more confident.*

And so ...
What could be an interesting new way to think about this?

> *What are different ways I could feel or become more confident?*

Thinking about what you want to change or transform....

Why?

Why?

Why?

**And so ...
What could be an interesting new way to think about this?**

TAKE A LONG BREAK HERE.

YOU CAN

EAT LUNCH.

GO FOR A STROLL.

PLAY WITH A PET.

STARE OUT THE WINDOW.

READ A POEM.

WRITE A POEM.

TAKE A NAP.

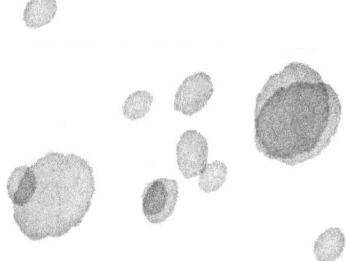

3

YOUR DAY: SYNTHESIZE
1-1½ HOURS

Let's take what we've done and bring it together in a way that can inspire you in your everyday life.

WRITE A LETTER FROM FUTURE YOU
45 MINUTES

Now that you're totally warmed up, let's dream of change and imagine your leap — big or small — and speak it into existence.

Visualize your aspirations with the power of a letter from the future — one written to present-day you... *from* **Future You**.

We'll do this in 5 paragraphs on the next few pages.

First, decide when and where **Future You** will be writing the letter. Will you be writing it from...

Next month?

Next year?

Five years from now?

A different city?

A new country?

A room in your home?

A favorite coffee shop?

What is the date of your letter?

Where will you be when you're writing it?

(1/5) Greeting and surroundings.

Address the letter to yourself and describe the first impressions you experience in a typical day in this future.

What does it feel like when you wake up in the morning in your new life?

Where are you?

What do you see out the window?

What does the air smell like?

What do you hear?

What are you wearing?

Who is nearby?

Dear _____ ,

This morning when I woke up...

(2/5) Where you started & why you made the change.

Think about your life as it is today and what factors inspired you to make a change in your life.

What "problem" were you trying to solve?

Why did you want to make a change?

What did you want to improve?

Writing as **Future You**, reflect on where you started and why you wanted to make a change in your life.

Here's an example:

> Last year I knew I had to get out of my bad job and do my own thing. The stress was not worth the pay and the cost to my mental health was too much. One day after a particularly challenging day, I'd just had enough and thought, "Something needs to change."

Last week / last month / last year, I...

(3/5) Connect the dots.

Put yourself in the shoes of **Future You**.

How did you get here?

What changes did you make?

What did you *do* to arrive at this **Future You**?

What happened or didn't happen?

What did you try?

What did you succeed (or fail) at doing?

Include a quote from a friend or loved one, something they might say about who or where you are as **Future You**.

Here's an example:

> I got the idea to start my own small business, doing what people always give me compliments on -- making birthday cakes. I was scared because I didn't know the first thing about business or if I could actually make money doing it. I took some online courses and started doing it after work. Starting with word-of-mouth from my friends, I'm now making a solid side income with plans to quit my main job soon. My new customer Rachel says my cakes are "better than anything in the local stores."

I started / got the idea / first tried...

(4/5) Describe details of this life.

From the point of view of **Future You**, talk about what you are planning on doing today in detail.

Include a quote from someone who knows or sees you in this future reality, e.g. a friend that tells you they're proud of or happy for you.

What are you doing today?

What are you excited about doing today?

What are you wearing today?

Who are you seeing today?

What are the glimmers that are true in this future reality?

What are you grateful for in this future reality?

Today I'm going to...

(5/5) Connections to others and what the world sees.

Think about the human and social world around **Future You** — friends, family members, colleagues, coworkers, teammates, clients, companions, neighbors, or anyone in your orbit.

Describe who you see, who sees you, how they see you, where they encounter you, or how you impact them or what you mean to their lives.

Who is around you?

What do you do with them?

Who are the other main characters in this future life?

How do they see you?

Which human connections spark the most happiness for you?

What good or meaningful things do you bring to the lives of those around you?

Today I'm going to see / call up / meet with...

And lastly, write a closing greeting and sign it.

Think about what closing thought **Future You** wants to give you. What would they say to you to inspire you to become them?

Then, sign it as you would any letter.

Here are some examples:

I believe in you,

I know you can do it,

Wishing this for you,

See you soon,

You've got this!

Finish your letter with a closing greeting and signature.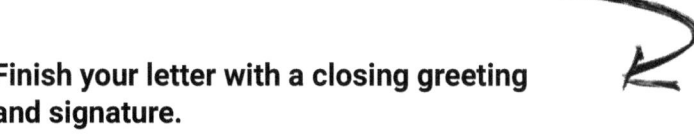

_____ ,

TAKE A SHORT BREAK HERE.

YOU CAN
HAVE A SNACK.
TAKE A SHORT WALK.
LIE ON YOUR BACK
AND
STARE AT
THE CEILING
OR SKY.

HOW MIGHT I.... ?
15 MINUTES

Ready for the final activity?

Imagining new paths or futures can be exciting but also intimidating. Where do you start? What small steps can you take to begin the journey?

Let's plant a seed that will help you grow into your future self. Visualizing and *being specific* about where to start can help put you on the path forward.

We'll do this through thinking: *How might I...?*

As in, how might you get answers to questions or other resources you need to take those first steps — and deciding *when* you'd like to do them by.

Try for two on the following pages after this example.

What questions do you need answers to?

What do you need to learn?

What resources do you need?

How do you get them?

When could you do or get them by?

Here's an example:

How might I...

Get healthier by eating better?

Idea(s) for where to start...

Find 3 new recipes and make them each 3 times.

Try a healthy meal delivery service for a month.

I could do this by this time...

2 months from now (my birthday)

How might I...

Idea(s) for where to start...

I could do this by this time...

How might I...

Idea(s) for where to start...

I could do this by this time...

CELEBRATE & EMERGE

You did it!

Congratulations on completing your sabbatical.

You...

Made a commitment to yourself and kept it.

Found time for your well-being.

Grounded yourself in your body.

Appreciated what you have.

Listened to yourself.

Let yourself dream.

Let yourself hope.

Imagined how you could grow.

And transformed how you see your life as you step back out into the world.

Now, before you get back out there...

TAKE A MOMENT TO...

TAKE A DEEP BREATH IN.

EXHALE.

STRETCH YOUR FINGERS AND TOES.

LOOK IN THE MIRROR

OR OUT THE WINDOW

AND SAY THANK YOU.

CLOSE YOUR EYES.

COUNT

10, 9, 8, 7, 6, 5, 4,

3, 2, 1

AND THEN

OPEN YOUR EYES.

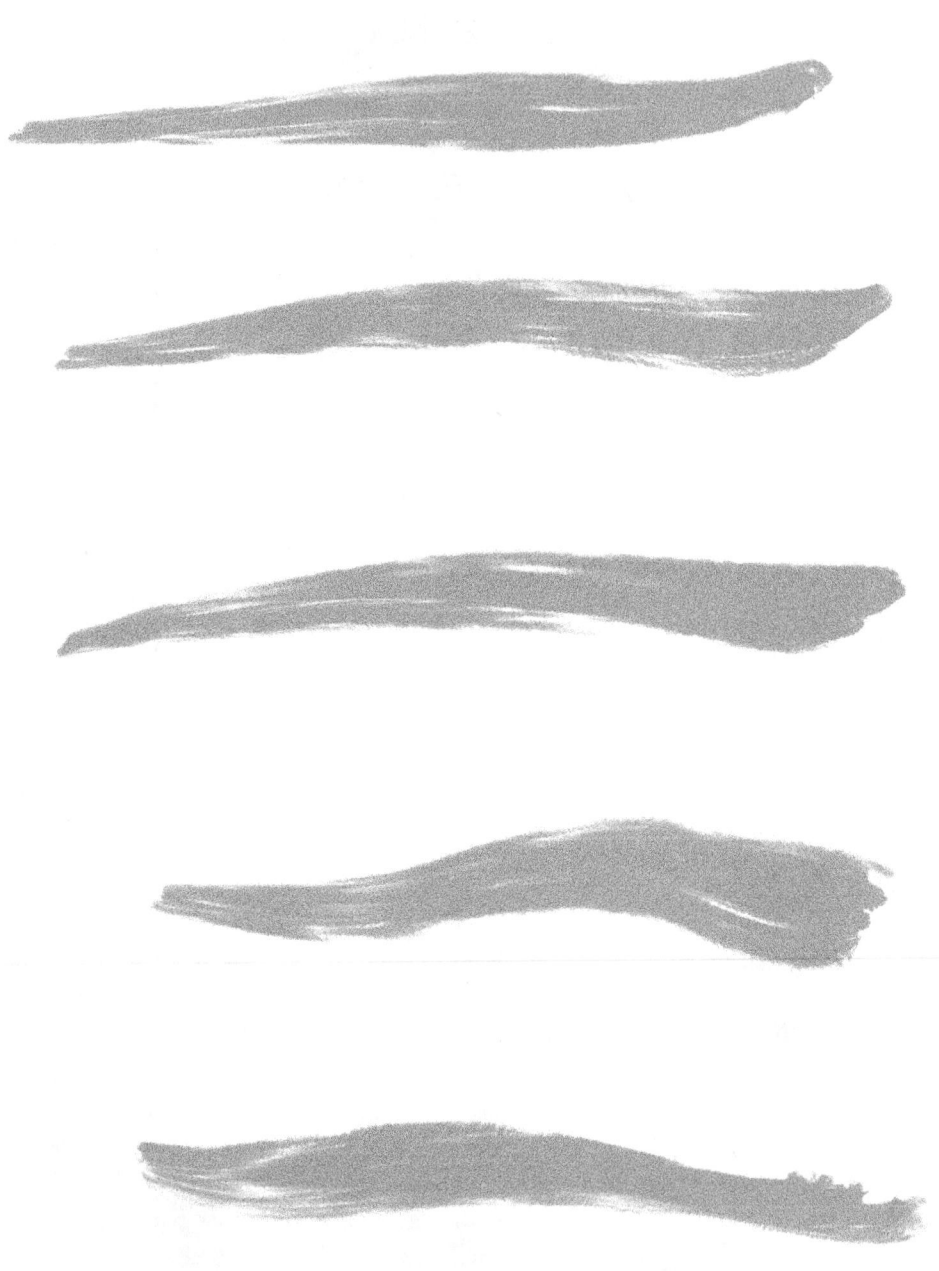

RESOURCES & REFERENCES

I'm always reading and compiling inspiring resources about sabbaticals and making space for creativity.

You can find these online @
one-day-sabbatical.com

This includes my own original article series that planted the seed for this book:

How to Sabbatical, Pt 1: Jump Off the Train
*How to Sabbatical, Pt. 2: F*ck It, I'm Going Around the World*
How to Sabbatical, Pt. 3: Re-Entry + What I Learned

References in this book

1. Schabram, K., Bloom, M., Didonna, DJ. (2023, February 22). Research: The Transformative Power of Sabbaticals. *Harvard Business Review.* https://hbr.org/2023/02/research-the-transformative-power-of-sabbaticals

2. Dalton-Smith, S. (2021, January 6). *The 7 types of rest that every person needs* [Video]. TED Conferences. https://ideas.ted.com/the-7-types-of-rest-that-every-person-needs/

3. Dana, D. (2018). *The Polyvagal Theory in Therapy: Engaging the Rhythm of Regulation.* W. W. Norton & Company.

ABOUT THE AUTHOR

Jill Corral is a design consultant, executive writing coach, photographer, and writer with 20+ years in innovation product design for companies such as Amazon, Sony Music, Teague, and Microsoft. In her work, she explores liminal states and inflection points — "in-between" places of change and reinvention in people's lives, society, technology, and art. She lives in Seattle, Washington with her wife Giti.

PHOTO CREDIT: AUTHOR

Find her online @
jill.design